Pub. by Imaginary World Comics
Printed in China
ISBN # 978-0-9822491-0-9

KALIEDOSCOPE

an assortment of comics,
photographs & artwork

featuring Mr Toast, Joe the Egg,
Shaky Bacon, Clem Lemon &
a host of other colorful characters

by Dan Goodsell
c. 2008

THE MYSTERIOUS MOEBIUS DONUT

THE FASCINATING
ANT FARM

SPOILT MILK

moogalicious

the letter "I"

knitwits

WATERMELON

You should chew before swallowing.

SUMO

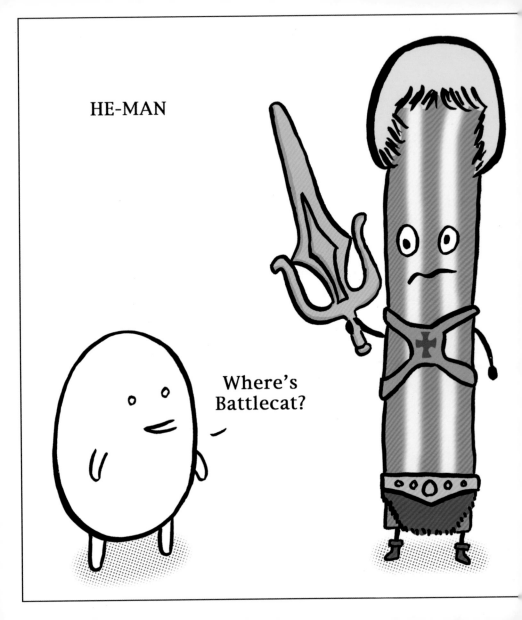

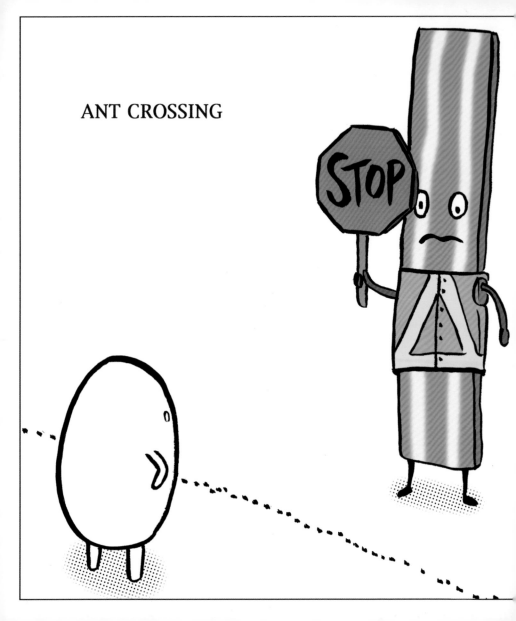

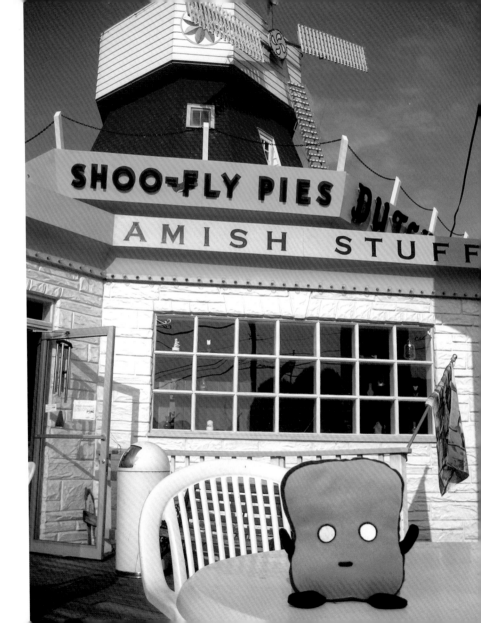

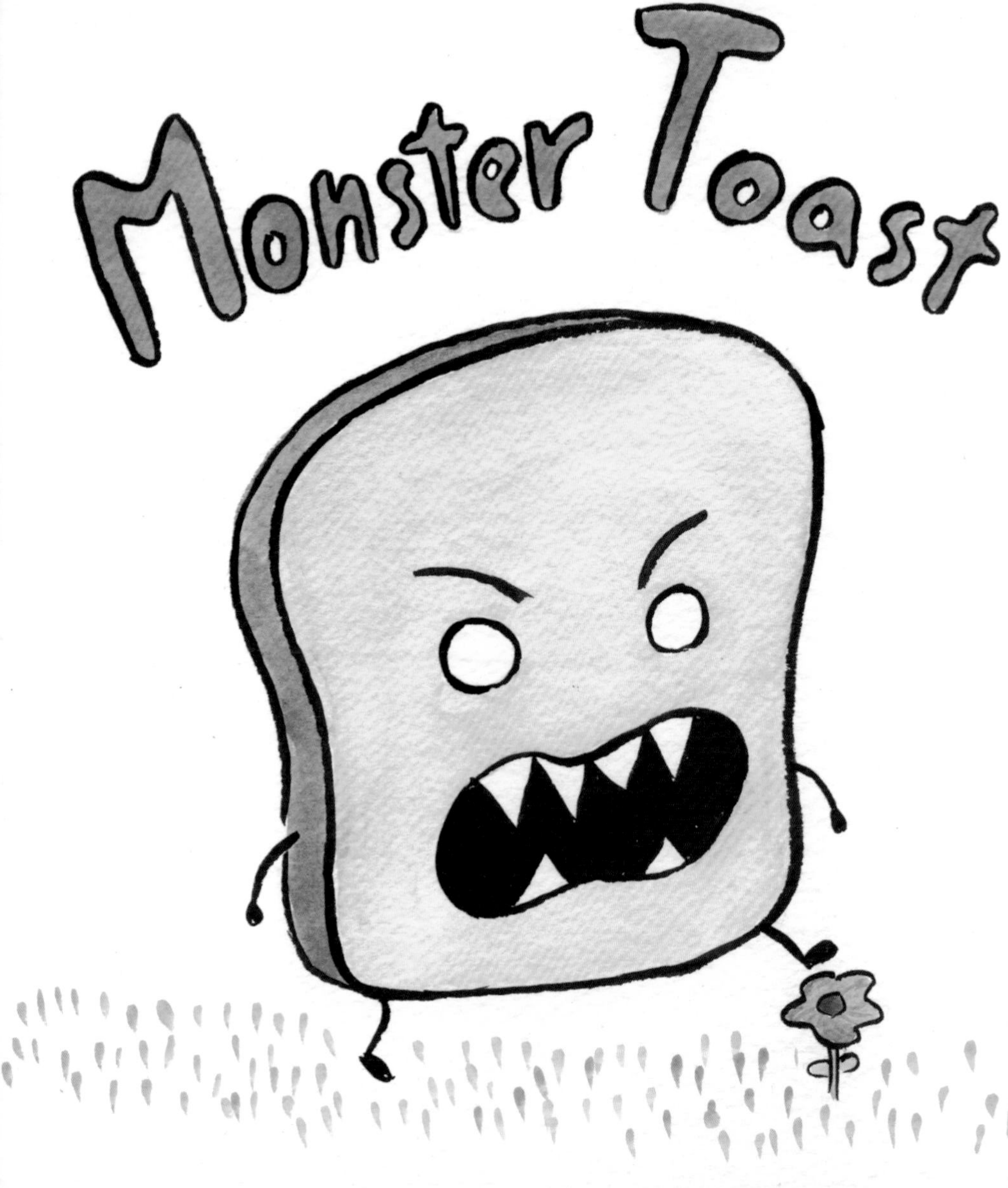
Monster Toast

LIMES

Catch the Pepper Train

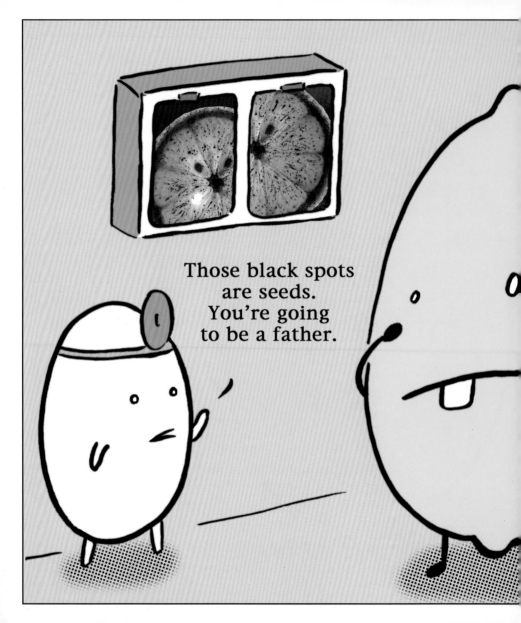

Somewhere there is a pig missin' his hat.

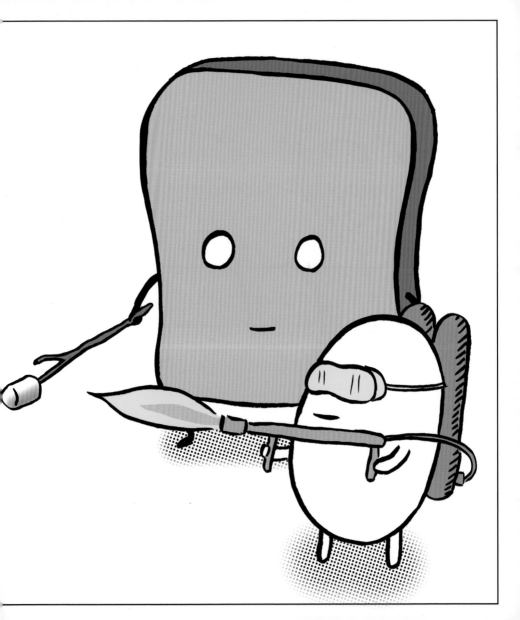

Oh little snail,
do you find
contentment
in your self
containment?

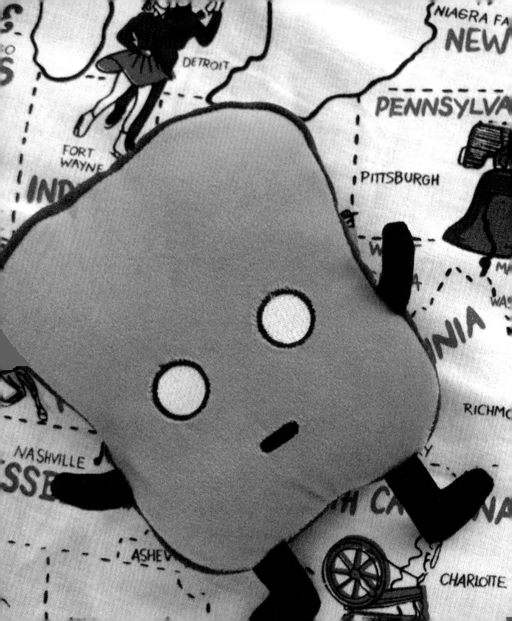

WINTER SCENES

Contents of this book are c. Dan Goodsell 2008.

Published by Imaginary World Comics, PO Box 48021
Los Angeles, CA 90048. Email to grickily@yahoo.com

Thanks to all the Mr Toast fans whose constant support keeps me going.

Photo credits - Modern Kitchen by Lala A. Gogo, Waffle House by Kirk Demarais,
Chopsticks by doc18, Shoo Fly Pies & State Map by Beth Lennon,
Shaky Snowball by Todd Franklin and Christmas Tree by Kirk Demarais.

Spider-Man is c. Marvel Comics, He-Man is c. Mattel & Super Mario is c. Nintendo.